THE STILLNESS *in the* RIVER

THE
STILLNESS
in the
RIVER

poetry to engage your soul

LANA LENSMAN

ISBN 979-8-9875062-4-0 (print)
ISBN 979-8-9875062-5-7 (e-book)

First Edition
Cover design by Holly Forrest

CONTENTS

SOJOURN 2

PREFACE

Soon after the publication of The Wind of Spoken
Words, I returned to the intimate conversation
with Spirit that birthed this poetry collection.
As I sat in silence with the next group of poems,
I noticed that the vibrational flow of the words
had changed. There seemed to be a progression
happening from one book to the next. I received
information that this series of poetry books mirrors
the awakening of consciousness.

In the first book, The Face in the Night Sky, we
are introduced to the soul journey. Following the
cycles of the moon, we are invited into the internal
landscape of Soul. We become aware of human
struggle: the seeking of perfection, the loneliness of
this seeking, and the strategies we devise to evade
our discomfort. We are guided inward to explore
and discover the reality of who we are. We receive
universal wisdom that inspires us to be still, silent,
present, and energetically contained.

In the second book, The Wind of Spoken Words,
we are shown the effects of carrying our past
stories into the future. We follow the "wind of our
words," we see where they land, and how

they create our reality. We delve deeper into the internal landscape of Soul, becoming more aware of our struggle. We follow the guidance to end the strategies that keep us stuck in the world of illusion. As we begin to apply universal wisdom in our lives, we find clarity on the path to soul evolvement.

In the third book, The Stillness in the River, the progression of soul evolvement becomes more apparent. Our attention turns to a greater vision of sustaining balance and harmony within the "flowing river of our lives." As a result, our understanding of universal wisdom deepens. We become aware of the gift of our bodies, our valuable connection to the earth, and our soul's desire to fulfill our destiny.

These books contain universal wisdom presented in poetic verse. The messages we receive resonate with our vibrational signature. We might not understand the words of a poem. We might even resist the words (this is highly valuable). Yet if we participate on any level, we are choosing to awaken our consciousness.

Close your eyes. Point your finger and touch the mandala.
Open your eyes to see the poem that wants to engage with you.
Each poem offers an entry point into the soul journey.
It will guide you inward, a slow spiral into the heart of creation.
Replicating nature's way, the energy of the mandala wants to
find center and then return, moving outward into life expression.

Center Point Soul Balance High or Low Life Stream Whole Being Kaleidoscope Destination Intersection Unwind Undercurrent High Rise The Air of Soul Inner Plame Five to Seven Earth's Power Jewel Treasure Den Jewel This Body Feelings I Love You Ease Freedom Responsible Effort or Action Reflection Unrevealed Rise Just Be Your Art Interference The Lion's Den Truth For Myself The Sacred Feel the Moment Whirling Dervish Take Flight The Embrace Watch Me The Storm Pure of Heart Move Lightly Swimming Soul's Recording The Edge Empty or Full Stop the Pain Hydrate My Soul Directs This Energy No Longer Tears Follow Me As I Am My Heart Right and Wrong Breath Travels The Unknown Man of Wisdom Return to You Moonflower Your Offering The Mirror

INTRODUCTION

The Stillness in the River invites you to move beyond time.

When you move beyond the stories in your mind of past and future, you enter the timeless realm of presence. You enter the atmosphere of Soul.

This poetry collection beckons you to find the center point within you, the deep well of stillness where presence is found. From this spaciousness, you can navigate the flowing river of your life with greater ease.

Whether you choose to use the mandala or open the book at random, each poem becomes the messenger of your present reality. As you explore the significance of the message, you bring soul wisdom into motion.

SOJOURN 1

center point

In equal measure
the pendulum
swings back and forth

The center point
is where time expands.

The weighted scale
is balanced
from left to right

The center point
is where time stands.

The stillness in the river
eventually becomes
a steady flow

The center point
is where time is known.

soul balance

When you rise above
into the realm of soul
with neglect of physical matter

Soul has no place
to land.

With too much focus
on earthly comfort
and physical needs

Soul has no space
to rise.

high or low

I

On Earth's surface,
water overflows
rivers run dry

wind is destructive
air stagnates

fire devastates
the world turns cold

either excess
or depletion
disrupts Earth's harmony

II

In the human body,
the high of emptiness
or the low of congestion
results in no flow

Within the mind,
an extreme view
or total disregard
results in no understanding

III

From the greater view,
within the flow of infinity
all lifecycles on Earth
remain in balance.

life stream

The momentum has been set.

There is a starting point
a chosen direction
the final destination

Your thoughts, your voice
your walk, your flow
direct what you seek
and where you go

Together, they become
your way of being,
the life stream
of your inner world.

whole being

Gather all the missing pieces
of your energetic presence

Call yourself back
from the people
who have taken
a part of you

Call yourself back
from the people
you have carelessly
given yourself to

Bring your mind and body
together with your soul
so that your life force
is flowing and strong

Return
to your whole being.

kaleidoscope

A colorful past merges
with the colors of the day
into the rainbow of the future.

Lifetimes blend
with one another
casting deeper hues,

the subtle tones
or vivid splashes
of your life.

As you evolve
you choose the colors
of your expression.

destination

I no longer need
to direct the way
choose the path
control the day

I can listen
without a doubt
and follow
the certain route

My clarity
of soul intention
will ignite
the destination

intersection

The point where two lives meet
is what you want to pay attention to.

It's the exact moment
you have been waiting for,

when the thread pulls tight
and soul knowing makes an appearance.

It is the center point
of perfect timing.

Arrive at this intersection
with deepest breath and grounded body.

Be still and listen
until it reveals your next step.

unwind

Unravel the day
you have become
entangled in

Smooth out the knots,
those moments
when the thread twisted

Notice the places
where you glided
around and through.

Unwind from the day
with gentle touch
and understanding,

until you reach
a state of ease
and hold a straight line.

undercurrent

The water is still
as I float
on its surface

yet I sense
an undercurrent
pulling me in

the water swells
and rises

in its depths
I swim

reaching for
what drifts by

layer upon layer
of beautiful truth

high rise

Don't expect to
take the elevator
to the top floor
right away.

Your mind
might be delighted
but your heart
will be amiss.

Only time and wisdom
will reveal
the higher levels
of Soul.

the air of soul

From above,
look below
take in the whole view

Notice what lingers
in the clouds
waiting to be dispersed

See what resides
at eye level
ready to meet you

or at least
catch your attention

And then,
look within your body
for the places without breath

Dialogue with them
connect deeply
feel and understand

Release the tension,
create the space
to open and expand

Explore the Air of Soul
but only after
you have spent time
with your earthly self.

inner flame

Beyond external form
into deep center
the flame of you exists.

Does your flame
burn bright,
high and still

or does it dim
and waver?

Watch over
your inner flame

Protect it
from too much wind
or drowning waters.

When you gaze inward
with a still mind,
you nourish soul's fire.

this body

My feet walk on ground
my hands swing in air
my legs take me places
my arms hold what's there

My head lifts towards sky
my tailbone touches earth
this body contains my soul
from the moment of my birth.

feelings

Feelings blow through
like the wind

They can float
on a gentle breeze
with subtle tones
of calm and ease

or abruptly
change direction
become fierce in voice
with strong inflection.

Feelings emerge
from deep earth

They can surface
like a mountain stream
with smooth textures
of peaceful dreams

or violently erupt
splatter and spark
clear the way
make their mark.

Feelings can either
drift in softly
or burst forth

They are nature
moving through us.

i love you

It's not the words you say
or the gifts you offer

It's not because
you show up
listen to me
pay my way
meet my needs

It's not because
you make me smile, laugh
and feel alive inside

I love you
because you are a soul
like me, traveling this earth,
and together
we meet our destiny.

ease

At the end
of the deep breath,

the moment
your body relaxes

or with the thought
that all is perfect
and there is enough

you will find
the center point
of ease

without tension
time expands
instead of demands

without resistance
space supports
instead of distorts

Body moves freely
Mind is receptive
Heart is open

the silence
in between each breath
reveals the ease of infinity

freedom

In opposition to
body's contraction
inner tension
and outer pull,

you will find Ease.

In opposition to
mind's rigidness
negative thinking
criticism and judgment,

you will find Open.

In the space
of ease and openness
in the space
of the redirect,

you will find Freedom.

responsible

See the many faces
of those who believe
they are responsible

the serious face
of the one
who must bear
the burden

the tired face
of the one
who conforms
to the rules

the righteous face
of the one
who always does
the right thing.

You can also find
many joyful faces

they are the ones
who are responsible
to their soul's calling.

effort or action

There is a difference
between effort
and action.

Action is the steady flow
of intention in motion
initiated by thought and feeling.

Effort is born from
internal resistance
to the tight pull of the external.

Action is neutral, present
driven by knowing.

Effort lives in the past
confused and entangled.

Replace effort with action
and you will return
to the straight line of ease.

reflection

Look around
and you will see
the reflection
of your inner being.

Before you judge,
remember
that what you see
in front of you

those things
you love
or hate,

each one
is a part of you
yet to be embraced.

unrevealed

One by one
they come together

a rhythm of numbers
revealed dreams
connecting words

Only a quiet mind
can hold the thread
long enough
to see where it leads

Too distracted
and the signs
lie dormant
unrevealed.

rise

Sit with your resistance
until you can say
Yes.

When you return
to the smooth flow
of deep knowing

Rise
once again.

just be

Here
Still
Listening

Just Be.

Feel
Earth

Absorb
Space

Sense
Soul

Just Be.

SOJOURN 2

your art

Creativity,
the effortless flow of soul
pouring through your veins

until you are so full
it has no choice
but to breathe out of you

it becomes your voice
your way of being
your art

interference

Find all the ways
you are pulled from
Center

Sense the disruption
to your way of
Being.

Notice the interference
the things that distract
your mind

and send your body

away

from

You

Clear up the confusion
the entanglements

that
wind
you
tight

Return
to the pure containment
of body and soul

earth's power

Fire burns bright
Wind is still
River flows strong
Earth grounds

Sentinel pines stand tall.

Aligned soul
Silent voice
Clear wisdom
Solid foundation

The Guardians are with you.

five to seven

I receive wisdom

my eyes observe
my ears listen
my nose detects
my mouth expresses

I inhale the new
I exhale the old

from crown to throat
before reach of heart

I smile
at the wonder
of it all.

truth

There is a place inside you
where Truth is crystal clear
and knowing flows strong

Within stillness,
you feel its weight, its ground
how it travels far to sky

Truth wants to emerge
from your mouth,
be seen in your ways

Let go of the layer of lies
placed upon you, and those
you have told and made yours

Truth is where
body and mind meet
and soul runs deep

Let your truth
travel freely

for myself

I don't need to be funny
act happy, appear smart
or look good
for you

I need to be myself.

I don't need to know
the right thing to say
give the best advice
or put my wants aside
for you

I need to free myself.

I don't need to stay quiet
hide my feelings
or speak certain words
for you

I need to be true to myself.

I don't need to do
what you want me to do
in the way you want me to,
do it, for you

My voice
My heart
My body
they belong to me

I choose to cherish myself.

the sacred

Timeless moment
with essence felt
light to the touch

So pure
senses still
words fall silent

feel the moment

Instead of moving on
to what's next,
feel the moment
breathe it in

Absorb it all
from head to toe
until it becomes
an even flow

Wait awhile,
before you speak it
before you write it
before you enter
time ahead

Feel the moment,
capture the fullness
contained within

Let it circulate
until it fills you
with the deepest truth

Appreciate
the density of feeling
your earth body offers.

whirling dervish

At the essence of heart's beat
the whirling dervish spins
with mysterious feat

Moving energy
round and round
at the center of infinity
until soul is found

Don't alter the flow
the speed or the depth
within the rotation
destiny is kept

take flight

Without worry
of what others see
what they believe
or how they perceive
you to be

Glide
wings spread wide
nothing to hide.

Without pressure
to achieve
to be seen
to realize a future dream

Soar
free of the before
and the stress
of needing more.

Without ties that bind
that pull or hold

Fly
in translucent skies
with open eyes
and no reprise.

the embrace

Finally arrived
to experience
the embrace
I have longed for

Surprisingly,
it is not the arms
of another
that holds me

It's an embrace
of a different kind,

where soul joins body
and heart's warm glow
penetrates deep inside

I am no longer reaching,

The One
reaches for me.

watch me

Go ahead, watch me
observe what I do

You can criticize
how I speak and act
the way I look
from front to back

but don't try to
define my words
hinder my feelings
direct my actions

You will never understand
the truth within me.

Don't put me in a box
you have left behind
or hold me in the past
as a story in your mind

The person you once knew
no longer exists,
she is free of your swipe
and your hiss.

I don't need you to tell me
how I should be

Nothing you say will sway
the deep love of self
I hold inside of me.

the lion's den

I expect you
to do something for me

Ahead of time
I'll throw out a line,
once you agree
you're no longer free

I have pulled you in
to the lion's den.

In the beginning
I'll give you some slack
but prepare for unhappy
if you decide to hold back

And I won't forget
what you did before

This time
if you don't follow through,
this lion will roar.

jewel treasure

Protect your innocence
it's a treasure.

A calypso orchid
peeking out from
the dense forest floor

rare
delicate
exquisite

Don't let anyone
who cannot see
trample it.

Of soft nature
with new eyes
be in the world

but protect this
jewel of heart.

pure of heart

The waters of grief
pour through you
absorbed by earth

The flames of rage
once ablaze
have turned to ash

Layers of understanding
blanket your heart

Be filled
with gratitude
for this cleansing

The return
to pure of heart
is celebrated

move lightly

I am simple
I am natural
I am pure of heart

I move lightly
in the world

No need to seek
possessions
achievement
social status

I shape my life
with eyes on inner heart
not outer world

Transparency is my art
the water runs clear
inside me

swimming

The wave I see
approaching

is Love
swimming
towards
Me

I greet her
with an open heart

I play
in her waters

soul's recording

Reciting poetry
written long ago
words memorized
in another time.

Faint glimpses
into this other world
fills the emptiness
once again.

Do these words I hear
pull me back in time
or is the future
drawing near?

Either way,
Soul's recording
continues on.

SOJOURN 3

the edge

You cannot grasp it
or even touch it
with your fingertips
but you can sense its
surrounding comfort
and hold it close.

At the edge of your energy field
tiny receptors engage
with the Universe

Your field knows
all that has been,
what is yet to come

It contains
the vibration
of your soul

As air caresses
and warmth permeates,
enjoy its presence

empty or full

What are you attempting
to fill up with?

Why do you fear
feeling empty?

If you have learned
to seek fullness,
then you view empty
as undesirable.

If you have learned
to seek emptiness,
then you view full
as unnecessary.

If you seek emptiness,
you are still attempting
to fill up with something.

Emptiness doesn't arise
from body's desire
or mind's direction.

What will the experience
of emptiness
fill you up with?

When you discover this,
your confusion will cease.

You will be filled
with inner peace.

stop the pain

I rush to the aide of others
when I sense the pain
they carry

I see the way
their actions
interfere with their soul

I want to fix it
I want to help them
I want to stop their pain

but if I take a moment,
turn inward,
I find the same pain
inside of me

Truthfully,
I am the one
I want to save.

If I turn towards myself
take the time to heal
not only will I be free

I will be able to understand
the pain of others

I will be able to understand
what it takes to change

Otherwise, the attempt
to stop their pain
so I do not feel my own
will continue.

hydrate

I

This energy I feel
it's bigger than me
I can't interfere
with its stream

a river of words
a current of truth
a wave of clarity

words swiftly fall
from higher rise
land before my eyes

it happens rather fast
a downpour of words
my mind wants to grasp

but these words I hear
from afar, that come near
have a mind of their own

II

This energy I feel
it's bigger than me
I can't interfere
with its stream

a soul dialogue
heard long ago
waiting to be written
in a perpetual flow

I am a sacred vessel
I fill, then empty

these words hydrate
those who are ready
to drink and absorb

my soul directs

My soul directs
my choices
not my mind

My soul directs
my actions
not by body

My soul leads me to
clarity of mind
harmony of body.

My mind supports
soul wisdom

My body supports
soul balance

My soul directs
my whole being,
with the power
to influence destiny.

this energy

I

In a wind tunnel
sitting at the center

This energy moves me
from deep inside
from the center point
flowing outward

I have a soul desire
to surrender

II

A cool spring
cascading down
from mountain crevice

gentle yet strong
soft yet direct
clear yet potent

This energy
nourishes and heals
the Earth

III

Emanating from
radiant galaxies
this energy awakens
the consciousness
of the Universe.

no longer

The pull of the unconscious
no longer leads me
away from my destiny.

My mind is receptive
it questions and explores
it no longer needs to know.

My body is wise
it listens and absorbs
it no longer needs to react.

When it feels right
when the pull is clear
when alignment appears,

my mind and body
support consciousness.

Only then, can my soul
travel through life with ease
towards destiny.

tears

Are these tears of joy
or tears of sorrow?

Sometimes it is hard to know
why tears arise,
they can catch you off-guard
be quite a surprise.

You can feel happy and sad
at the same time,
without even knowing
what's held in your mind.

Your tears can reveal
something down deep,
a message from Soul
that wakes you from sleep.

If you follow your tears
to the place where you hold,
if you stop and you listen
there's a story to be told.

So, sit with yourself
don't let your mind stray,
hear your cry, hear your voice
until your tears wash away.

the storm

When the clouds darken
and the rain pours down
from your broken heart

When the lightning strikes
and breaks open
your hidden pain

Search for
the center of stillness,
the calm breath
of Soul.

Be still through the storm
until you can inhale
the fresh air
of the Sacred.

complicated

Mind leads us astray
Body resists
Soul becomes lost

Seems like human life
is complicated...
or is it?

Go back to the beginning

Listen to what your mind
is telling you

Understand what lies behind
your body's resistance

Connect with your soul

The unacknowledged
what's hidden within,
makes your life
complicated.

my heart

Many hearts grasp for me,
they want me to soothe
their pain

but I am here
for my heart
in this moment

I saturate
my heart
with Love

The days of filling up
the hearts of others
while mine sits empty
are over

With a full heart
I radiate love
to the whole world

return to you

Hands on heart
eyes turned inward

Return to You

Hold yourself close
Wash away others
Be with your soul

Feel the places
in your body that yearn
to speak with you

Sink into your own arms
to receive the eternal
embrace

Return to You

right and wrong

I

I don't need to be right
I need to be true

to my voice
to my heart
to my soul.

Behind my need
to be right
is the fear of
being wrong

yet the truth is,
right and wrong
are intertwined.

II

Sometimes,
you need to be wrong
to understand
what is right

When you explore
what went wrong
you learn,

who you are now
who you want to become.

Beyond your mind's view
of right and wrong
you uncover truth

You experience
freedom.

the unknown

My body reveals
the pull of Destiny…
it's reaching for me

If I follow
I will arrive
in the unknown

With a clear mind
and open heart
I say, *Yes*

follow me

I cannot meet you
where you are
instead, rise up
to meet me

Follow me
into shimmering stars
of highest skies
where the Divine
is at rest

as i am

Know me
as I am

still
clear mind
calm body
aligned soul

See me
as I am

active
conditioned mind
earth-worn body
an identity

Love me
as I am

present
wise mind
soulful body
innocent

moonflower

When light fades
and dark saturates
the night sky,
you bloom.

Moonflower,
teach me your ways.
Keep me from closing
tight in the dark.

Help me to blossom
in the pain of night,
when tears fall
and I cannot bear
the path ahead.

Teach me
how to reach for
the healing
of the moon.

breath travels

Eyes closed
Deep breath

I am here
I am listening

Inner gaze
Breath travels

I am here
I feel you

Eyes open
Calm breath

I am here
I know you

man of wisdom

Stands tall as ancient pines
with flow from earth to sky

You will sense
the eternal flame
burning bright
as his wisdom ignites.

For those who are ready
to expose their heart
to the flame,

the hawk will soar
with straight flight
into your pain.

And when the voices
of the lost
sing once again,

you will remember
the Man of Wisdom
and how it all began.

your offering

Let the stories of your past
of your woes and your strife
be absorbed by the earth
as you plant a new life.

Let the burdens of your heart
that have stifled your breath
be carried to soul waters
and set gently adrift.

Let the fear in your body
that dampens life's stride
be diffused into light
as food for the skies.

Then, with enlightened
pure state of being,
let peace and clarity
be your offering.

the mirror

You can look in the mirror
to see yourself
but what you will see
staring back at you
is only the surface layer

it will never reflect the beauty
of your true essence

You can look within
to see a clear reflection of you
and as you lose focus
on the outer image
and how others view you

you will see yourself
as whole and perfect

ABOUT THE AUTHOR

I revel in my walk with soul, my body grounded to earth, with my sight on the moon. When I am not in dialogue with Spirit, writing, or guiding others you will find me in nature walking and listening. – Lana Lensman

www.ingramcontent.com/pod-product-compliance
Lightning Source LLC
Chambersburg PA
CBHW020754130626
46554CB00006B/2188